NOT YET HUMAN

A PREPONDERANCE OF
APHORISMS TO PONDER

DAVID L. LAING

Cosmic Art Center

Published in the United States of America

Cosmic Art Center

8903 35th Avenue NE

Seattle, Washington 98115

Paperback ISBN 978-1-960089-01-4

Ebook ISBN 978-1-63944-910-1

CONTENTS

APHORISM

a concise statement of a principle;
a terse formulation of a truth or sentiment
—Merriam-Webster Dictionary

FOREWORD

David L. Laing's mind overflows with images and ideas. Often that boundless creativity manifests as drawings, sometimes as articles, occasionally as novels. Most recently, hundreds of aphorisms have gushed forth, enough to fill four books. This is the first.

Maybe, like many of us, you first learned about aphorisms in high school English class, studying Shakespeare's *Julius Caesar*. One of the most memorable aphorisms is, "The evil that men do lives after them; the good is oft interred with their bones."

David's aphorisms are in a much different vein. As with his other writings, they may touch on unexpectedly various themes. They may be metaphors or conundrums, wise or humorous. They are presented not by theme or concept, nor grouped in any order, just poured out as they sprang to

David's mind. As in his books of articles, the *Beyond the Box* series, the organization is randomness.

The 750 aphorisms in this book are meant to be pondered, as its subtitle expresses, rather than devoured in a gulp. Take your time here. Dip in now and then. Ponder, reflect, contemplate. Come back again later for a few more gems.

Back to Shakespeare, another aphorism from *Julius Caesar* reflects David's spirit amazingly well:

"It is better to create than to learn! Creating is the essence of life."

NOT YET HUMAN

APHORISMS

—1—

One sings to order things.

—2—

The triumph of Mars is celebrated
with a trumpeter.

—3—

Voice of the Muse is amusing
not confusing.

—4—

It takes *guts* to play the violin.

—5—

In flight from boredom,
find the kingdom of light.

—6—

God of Art is hidden, not bidden
and comes when ridden.

—7—

Pearls in perils.

—8—

The right sound can change
the nature of the ground.

—9—

Beauty is a state
belonging to its own country.

—10—

Musical mandala is a sound kabbalah.

—11—

Equestrians are not pedestrians—
some horses have wings.

—12—

Traverse an oceanic valley
to the sound steersman of a moving galley.

—13—

Deepen is better than improve,
taking below what was above.

—14—

There is truth at the bottom of foolishness
and foolishness at the bottom of truth.

—15—

Suffering is relative, pleasure absolute.

—16—

We live only one verse
in the poem of the universe.

—17—

Train to be the train to leave both station
and stationary.

—18—

Ideal university is real diversity of one.

—19—

Wield the pen, yield to zen.

—20—

Be the sphere to be complete here.

—21—

The definition of "ecstasy"
is to stand outside oneself.

—22—

Enlightenment turns
a staircase into an escalator.

—23—

In the not so remote past getting stoned
meant death, not getting high.

—24—

Unstable by nature, the artist is still capable
of painting a picture.

—25—

A name is a flame, claim to fame
and a word game.

—26—

The novel is already novel—just write it.

—27—

The three-legged stool is no fool.

—28—

We accept defeat
before the world can accomplish the feat.

—20—

Clever is a lever that can raise up
a wise man forever.

—30—

The trinity resounds through the triangle.

—31—
Rather than believing in the gods
and admiring the self, admire
the gods and believe in the self.

—32—
Trapped in the intellect
it is not possible to reflect.

—33—
A true revolutionary acts in ways
that are not revolutionary, but *evolutionary*.

—34—
When quantity and quality
take on characteristics of each other,
a discovery has been made.

—35—
Madness is one fountain of knowledge
among many to attain.

—37—
Loss of temper is a lapse in humor
from a conflict of *humors*.

—38—
Dig the novel with a metaphysical shovel.

—39—

Force of beauty is its own source.

—40—

Spirit is Scripture.

—41—

Reality is no joke,
which is why it is so funny.

—42—

If it happened in history it's a story,
if it happens now it's history.

—43—

Panic is at the opposite ends of panoramic.

—44—

The sense of beauty is a potent weapon
that thrills rather than kills.

—45—

The purpose of sex
Is not to give life meaning
but to free the mind to find it.

—46—

An eternal foe is anyone or anything
that lacks Imagination from tip to toe.

—47—
Happiness is to not miss what is missing
and kiss what is not missing.

—48—
Distaff is your better half
no matter how you spin it..

—49—
Galactic man has an astrological address
more or less.

—50—
Flower, tower, power.

—51—
Own tone to hone the stone.

—52—
Humor will not save the world,
but it will save those who will.
The world will be saved by Art.

—53—
I don't choose a time to write.
The words choose their time
to write me.

—54—

Unafraid of death
is different from being unafraid of dying.

—55—

Compress time into space to produce
a theater of grace.

—56—

The mirror is a mirage.

—57—

Ask Dance to make a mask.

—59—

Truth cannot distinguish
between art and knowledge.

—60—

Tears of sadness
quench fears of madness.

—61—

In ancient times it was up to the scribe
to decide what to describe.
The diatribe has no tribe.

—62—

To become whole is the goal of the soul.

—63—

Life on Earth is the story of a long struggle
to see who, in the end, will brainwash who.

—64—

Cymbals clash with all other instruments.

—65—

Middle name of the planet is Middle Earth.

—66—

Saw! It cuts through something,
enabling the sawyer to see.

—67—

United with space, there is *time*
to see an angel face at the end of the race.

—68—

Restore ore to the core
of the emotional store.

—69—

Instruction is the shape of construction.

—70—

A *vision* is a bird's eye view
with no self-division.

—71—

Silence the sound, hear the music.

—72—

Forego the ego and go.

—73—

A good preacher is an unsuccessful teacher.
A good teacher is an unsuccessful preacher.

—74—

To be happy is not *being* happy.

—75—

In prison there is one color,
through the prism there are many.

—76—

Don't mutter or stutter—
sing the utter truth.

—77—

Art is a creative act of fiction or fact.

—78—

A peak took a peek at itself and melted.

—79—

Earth's favorite emotion is mirth.

—80—

Mars dreams of orange stars.

—81—

The right word is a sword
that cuts to the world.

—85—

Unravel what's at hand,
travel to a new land.

—86—

Who complains misunderstands
the magical properties of brains.

—87—

Insights began through ancient pagan rites.

—88—

Inspiration comes from respiration.

—89—

A saxophone is a telephone that makes
a person-to-person call to one and all.

—90—

Writing is an intuitive way
of fighting with better lighting.

—91—

Drinking stops thinking.
Thinking stops drinking.

—92—

Chose to overdose,
hope is potent dope.

—93—

Fog clears, god steers.

—94—

March is on its spring march.

—95—

Ideal waiter serves to wait.

—96—

Way of the river is to wind;
way of man is to find
what not to leave behind.

—97—

Though truth is always present
it can never be made a present.

—98—

Fate lies somewhere between
understate and overstate.

—99—

A pitcher's mound
is the raised game's holy ground.

—100—

Royalty in aesthetics demands total loyalty.

—101—

The X factor *is* an inner actor.

—102—

A many-sided head
is a diamond cut never in a rut.

—104—

In search of himself,
the hunter is always the hunted.

—105—

Being stronger, the ship at sea takes over—
ultimate mutiny.

—106—

When the sky plots its own course
it is at its source.

—107—

We did not ask to be free,
which is why we are here on this wild spree.

—109—

A prophet never profits from the mistakes
of others—he prophesies them.

—110—

Will is a deep well.

—111—

Quicksand is faster than the speed of hand.

—112—

Know is to grow. Ask the trees.

—113—

Waterfall for all to show the rainbow.

—114—

Cascade is a parade.

—115—

Indigenous Socrates: Know your*selves*,
arranged vertically like a totem.

—116—

Precision is the true mother of invention—
it's necessity's decision.

—117—

Art frames meaning.

—118—

Prison: A moment of indecision.

Freedom: Precision of the moment.

—119—

Love: To be at one with all that is
here-below and above.

—120—

Belief is relief from grief.

—121—

The world is a tarot card.
Know how to read each shard.

—122—

Strum the drum, ring the string,
hear the bell sing.

—123—

It is not how well you play the instrument
but how well it plays you.

—124—

Transcendence is independence.

—125—

One of the binary stars will eventually
catch the other: love from above.

—126—

Visions of the visionary:
What the mind sees that the eyes don't.

—127—

Anxiety: Temporary amnesia
of self-knowledge.

—128—

Pessimism and optimism are defined
by the awareness of the other.

—129—

Spine has 33 notes all in a melodic line.

—130—

The Artist believes that his art
will save the world,
though not necessarily *this* world.

—131—

Harmony of the spheres is a circle of fifths.

—132—

For life swans mate—
king and queen checkmate.

—133—

Coffee grounds for the not grounded.

—134—

As lower needs are fulfilled
higher ones are not automatically billed.

—135—

A play without *play* is mere display.

—136—

Love is not made but created—
more objet d'art
than wedding cake conflated.

—137—

Hate is love that arrived too late.

—138—

Are most schools of thought
just the thought of fools?

—139—

Master and slave are both master and slave
to each other.

—140—

Sensuality is not something to be revealed,
but unveiled.

—141—

When an idea is sound, you hear it.

—142—

Energy at one with its own synergy.

—143—

Non-human and human are connected
and separated by a hyphen.

—144—

A human climbs the divine vine.

—145—

Known for falling off its edge,
the limits of knowledge are shown as a ledge.

—146—

Plants' sexual relation to the world
is their root of constant elation.

—147—

Desire to emerge from the mire
is what catches fire.

—148—

Believe you are a sieve.

—149—

Key to self-preservation:
w*hole* observation.

—150—

A clown will never drown in a frown.

—151—

On a whim to swim, dive into divinity.

—152—

To bear the burden of free choice
needs a highly unique tone of voice.

—153—

The purpose of a big city
is to be the obstacle to overcome adversity.

—154—

There is no better hobby
than complete awareness of the body.

—155—

A true aim should never be confused
with claim to fame.

—156—

A lone wolf will in the end be rewarded
for its howl, though for now
does not know how.

—157—

Infused and fused, not confused.

—158—

Scoring is a temporary antidote
to all that is boring.

—159—

Once it is found
the human mind is a great find.

—160—

Way of the saint is to pray and paint.

—161—

Ill is the opposite of will.

—162—

Deep sleep undertaken is safe,
the nightmare begins
when you dare to awaken.

—163—

Immortality is not fatal.

—164—

Thirst: Unacceptance of life as desert.

—165—

Oasis is dessert for the deserted
in the desert.

—166—

The pinot noir grape is a role model to ape:
craving the most difficult terrain
to produce the best wine for the brain.

—167—

Harboring self-doubt, sail into the sea
of knowledge to see what it is about.

—168—

Supernatural is understood
through superconsciousness.

—169—

Blood to wine—elixir for the divine.

—170—

Internal struggle, external juggle.

—171—

To fall in love helps to *stand* oneself.

—172—

Body serves the Mind
though the Mind is not yet its master.

—173—

Peace eliminates
the pleasure of warrior states.

—174—

Only war worth winning
is waged against oneself.

—175—

Sweat of toil reveals
the sweet fruit of soil.

—176—

Though not officially cave-dwellers,
we are still trying to emerge
from its dark cellars.

—177—

Woman is the oil in the car called man.
Don't let it get dirty
and it won't need to be changed.

—178—

In love, a woman who is not sm*art*
as well as strong will not last long.

—179—

What is genius? Finding the right object
to communicate *you* as subject.

—180—

Control emotion by controlling motion.

—181—

The only function of an order is to give
the illusion that there is no disorder.
True order cannot be commanded.

—182—

An adult, still a child,
is not yet a grown-up.

—183—

Those who don't apply art exactly
as they were taught are pretty smart.

—184—

Convention can only be countered
by invention.

—185—

Never too late to save yourself
from a stored life on the shelf.

—186—

History is his or her story.

—187—

Trapped in a terrestrial envelope,
stamped celestial.

—188—

A woman destroys a man forgetting that
she could have also created him.

—189—

Acquire willpower to require
an uphill climb to its tower.

—190—

After we die we don't go anywhere,
we go everywhere.

—191—

Left in cold storage
the Spirit can continue to store its rage.

—192—

With no aim, how can we stake our claim?

—193—

Savor your savior.

—194—

What is contained in books is also
in brooks. Its knowledge meanders around
each reed, drop by drop to read.

—195—

Sword-fighting, to fencing,
to classical ballet—fight enlightens dance.

—196—
Creativity is the only true mirror.

—197—
Man is a horse,
mounted by its own spirit in full force.

—198—
First principle of the Universe is number
and its *one* song is the gong.

—199—
We are a ladder where each rung
is a ring to fight until hearing the bell ring.

—200—
Hell: A world without Art;
Heaven: A world where each plays
his or her creative part.

—201—
Exhaustion: Only one part
of machinery is overworked.

—202—
A straitjacket is always crooked.

—203—
To walk on water changed to wine
become serpentine.

—204—
Traveling abroad broadens
the horizontal code.
Traveling the home mental *road*
heightens the vertical mode.

—205—
Willing to willfully will
the contrary to being still.

—206—
Live up to the name and book cover
or game over.

—207—
Enhance romance with a glance,

—208—
Getting old is not bold when told
to despise a surprise.

—209—
Each *letter* is written to get better.

—210—
To lead through the mess,
messiah has a message for the age.

—211—

A well-placed verb can be as medicinal
as a powerfully curing herb.

—212—

On the brink, no time to think,
pray to many gods.

—213—

Harassed by the past
fail to make the present last.

—214—

A virtuous man does not value his virtues,
they value him.

—215—

Truly naked is well-dressed,
the opposite is also true.

—216—

A free man full of everything but himself
never feels empty.

—217—

The conventionally successful
stops growing when convinced
weaknesses are strengths.

—218—

Each day *eman*ates its ray.

—219—

Shame is finding someone
or something to blame.

—220—

Body as tool is the ultimate school.

—221—

Body and Imagination
form one united nation.

—222—

Optimism is to touch,
not be out of touch.

—223—

No easy relief on the hard road to belief.

—224—

Voice can only rejoice out of its box.

—225—

Cock crows because it knows
it cannot fly like a crow.

—226—
To head in the right direction
depends as much on the body as the head.

—227—
In error a comet burns itself out in terror.

—228—
A star falls unable stand
the pressure when the cosmos calls.

—229—
Ask the tire if God is pressure.

—230—
We are *not* born free but in chains—
take control of the reins.

—231—
Because the earth is round
go underground to feel it all around.

—232—
See beauty where it is
and *will* it where it isn't.

—233—
Neglect the contented worshiping
of the cow. Select the cat
as the sacred animal now.

—234—

An ideal mate does not make you
too happy to create.

—235—

On personality prison parole,
stay in the role you control.

—236—

Authentic education lubricates the part
that starts with the arts.

—237—

What book besides yourself
can change your outlook?

—238—

Change the word, change the world.

—239—

Let magic conjure up the image,
believe in the mage.

—240—

Editing is meditating.
Meditation is edition.

—241—

Soul is a battleground
between chaos and sound.

—242—

If someone just told you they saw
a cow fly over a house,
would you ask what color
or say it impossible?

—243—

Only escape from the reality cape
is a new shape to undrape.

—244—

Similar to an airplane, Imagination carries
the mind in another plane.

—245—

For the foundation of society
to be questioned
mind must be found to be unsound.

—246—

Dawn of a new kingdom
is not visible through the yawn of boredom.

—247—

Born in a manger, genius is a danger.

—248—

Intuitive tower topples over into clover
from a power failure of the mind
saying it's over.

—249—

That part that seeks to abort
will desire more comfort.

—250—

Picture the world as one grand opus
through a wide- angle focus.

—251—

A man of this world
creates a new one with the Word.

—252—

Don't strangle the intuition
to untangle a situation

—253—

Solomon is a continent king,
not a solo man.

—254

At a target of concentric circles
and ever-widening eccentric cycles
the Giant Archer shoots *arrow-man.*

—255—

Play in the key of "Be."

—256—

Mount a horse to ride without remorse.

—257—

For one who *understands*

much energy is released through the hands.

—258—

We fear what we are unable to hear.

—259—

Urges to travel

surges from a mind ready to unravel.

—260—

Is the mammoth wedding cake

of civilization ready to bake

a monumental mistake?

—261—

Search again and again—research.

—262—

An imposter has incorrect posture.

—263—

Dam the stream-of-consciousness

into a manmade lake

is an unnatural remake.

—264—

A slave and a master

both possess the other inside, undercover.

—265—

Live through the age of musical sabotage.

—266—

Love is a wild horse untrained
to pull a marriage carriage through
heaven and hell regardless of the age.

—267—

Be your own master—go slow, it's faster

—268—

House is like the body.
Do you own it or does own you?

—269—

It is interesting to *note* that "do,"
the first note of the musical scale,
is the same spelling as *do*—
something.

—270—

The missing link is to how to think.

—271—

Take up the *sax* to relax.

—272—

Contained in the musical scale
is a description of the world as a sound tale

—273—
The songbird belts out its song
to find its place in the winged throng.

—274—
Reality is unaccustomed
to its own costume.

—275—
Worth more than a token,
words are wisdom in how they are spoken.

—276—
Pill is taking the place of
the church on the hill.

—277—
View the world through a "macroscope"
rather than a microscope.

—278—
The hunter prays that the prey
is not himself.

—279—
Discover in the dark woods light moods.

—280—
Opening doors to other rooms—
the flower blooms.

—281—

Do you identify with a saucer if it's flying?

—282—

Don the robes of sunset or of dawn.

—283—

The *fort* of comfort protects us
from development—it's imprisoning.

—284—

As its own fertilized land
sensuality can be cultivated by hand.

—285—

The difference between childlike
and childish is more will than wish.

—286—

A *visionary* re-orders normal mental order.

—287—

Love is not something to play with—
it plays with you.

—288—

Loss of sense over nonsense makes sense.

—289—

It is wise to bet on Tibet.
Win or lose you get high.

—290—

Not immune to Nature,
commune with yourself—naturally.

—291—

Sitting high up in a tree, find your own
branch of knowledge to set you free.

—292—

Whatever God or gods
mapped out the universe,
rose to compose prose as well as verse.

—293—

A tree is as interesting as the number three.
Its divinity is in its trinity of
root, branch and fruitful infinity.

—294—

Run it up the chain
as if a cloud were recalling its rain.

—295—

Sacrifices suffice to eliminate vices.

—296—

A great liquid hand waves to the sand.

—297—

Self-contempt is the enemy
of a fresh attempt.

—298—

Look yonder and feel stronger longer,

—299—

The secret to energy in excess
is a peak experience success.

—300—

Dance to fight and fight to dance.

—301—

A sculpture is what remains
of its original picture.

—302—

The obvious is bidden to remain hidden.

—303—

Only the puzzle pieces mattered
after the world mirror shattered.

—304—

Simplicity is a whole-in-one complexity.

—305—

Each cobblestone is cobbled together
to build a throne of stone.

—306—

A spinet sounds the way you spin it.

—307—

Let the violin play in the key of violet.

—308—

An organ can't be transplanted
nor be a donor—play it with honor .

—309—

A flute softens the soul of a brute.

—310—

In the middle of the riddle
lies the key to the fiddle.

—311—

Pluck the strings of the Harpsichord
to dispel discord.

—312—

Viola is the middle name
of the classical trio.

—313—

Oblivious inside the obvious likes to hide.

—314—

In fear to appea,r danger is not always near.

—315—

Actively brainwash yourself
in your own spin cycle
or be passively brainwashed
by others caught in their dry circle.

—316—

Folklore is a philosophical core.

—317—

The brain can gain
with just the right amount of pain.

—318—

Sorrow fits into narrow
as laughter into larger.

—319—

The mind is a kind of mine.

—320—

Body-Mind continuum
fills Mankind's vacuum.

—321—

The stage is the brain, the play is pain.

—322—

Loss of nerve can cause a swerve
when navigating a dangerous curve.

—323—

Genius is its own aegis.

—324—

Without the right wife,
an uncertain life can become purely strife.

—325—

Whatever religion, system or creed
that bans humor cannot succeed.

—326—

Shifting the body into gear
is not always as easy as it might appear.

—327—

Development can be pushed
but never rushed. Build the fort
to defend through daily effort.

—328—

Did you discover it or did it uncover you?
The discoverer is often the recoverer.

—329—

Filled with imaginary toys, the playroom
in the house of the mind is a reality of joys.

—330—

Discover the brain pretending to be insane.

—331—

A universal language would be an art book
understood with a prolonged look.

—332—

True magic is rejected in its essence
before having a chance
to make its presence.

—333—

Incarceration—the car
cannot move on its own.

—334—

Are the mourners mourning for the dead
or for their own life ahead
that fills them with dread?

—335—

Uncertainty is more certain
in its uncertainty than certainty is
in its certainty.

—336—

Wizards and magicians were persecuted
because their knowledge came
through intuitions and not institutions.

—337—

The world becomes different
and more alluring
when the invisible turns visible.

—338—

Mars is too distant to be marred.

—339—

Thinking cap and celestial cape,
the Mind readies for escape.

—340—

Unhappiness is worn on the sleeve
of pleasure-seekers unwilling to believe.

—341—

The fishing boat at sea is stronger
than the fisherman can see.

—342—

Unaware of a state of despair
there is nothing to repair.

—343—
Next to its script
the Mind completes the text.

—344—
Radiating multiple charms,
the mermaid swallowed
the sun's thousand arms.

—345—
Take the bait or just cling and wait.

—346—
Certain pagan rites can be far less primitive
than *civilized* religious rights.

—347—
Thinking you are happy or sad
is a luxury of the unoccupied and mad.

—348—
"Mahalo" is the ultimate halo.

—349—
Trust the brain to create a brain trust.

—350—
Who is to say the average navvy
is not the most savvy.

—351—

Saxophones grew from the roots of trees
with earth tones blowing the breeze.

—352—

It is not a question
of how one becomes a visionary,
but how the visionary becomes One.

—353—

The Spirit prefers the marathon
even though the sprint is more spirited.

—354—

The one old rock that is not a rolling stone
is the *bolder.*

—355—

Hammer the human sentence
into its own grammar.

—356—

Each stone has its signature tone,
each tone a sign to be born.

—357—

Train a tree with rain.

—358—

The anatomy of astronomy we trust
is purely stardust.

—359—

Paradise found is purgatory bound.

—360—

See light become *light.*

.

—361—

The only difference between the arrow
and the ray is one is lighter.

—362—

Art cost what love lost.

—363—

Noosphere is not new here

—364—

The only card that can't be played is wild:
the joker.

—365—

Cosmos wears a long green cape
that opens for stars to escape.

—366—

Laughter out of control has a sacred role.

—367—
Maturity: take the good with the bad
to not go mad.

—368—
Patience is the most advanced science.

—369—
In the land where light rays slanted,
men are seeds to be planted.

—370
Standing apart doing art
make the world take part.

—371—
After Daniel left the lion's den
he became a teacher of men.

—372—
Uncover the brain,
discover knowledge drops of rain.

—373—
Plight of the search for light
is by night and by flight.

—374—
Not worth its weight in gold,
the spirit's height cannot be bought or sold.

—375—

Not at rest but still in the chest is the rest.

—376—

Surmount anything
to amount to something.

—377—

Knowing everything he does *not* know
makes him wise.

—388—

To keep spirit and soul intact
became an autodidact.

—389—

The demiurge has a housewife
whose home is this "world-maid."

—390—

Good taste in music
cannot be gotten in haste.

—391—

The angel of the lord said,
"Behold, I am with you."
But forgot to add:
"Hold your own till I can get there."

—392—

To build a new world,
start with a house and a garden.

—393—

Be bullet, trigger and gun—
do your own shoot just for fun.

—394—

Route to fortune is right routine.

—395—

Birth is any moment of mirth
and can even happen here on earth.

—396—

Hell is a mental state
not determined by fate.

—397—

The original scripture written on a scroll
explained a world on a roll.

—398—

Precision is the correct decision.

—399—

In a pure state, do nothing but elate.

—400—

In the world of aleatory,
there is no story nor glory.

—401—

Karl had nothing in *commune*
with the Marx Brothers .

—402—

Numb as well as dumb,
the soul with no fire has nowhere to aspire.

—402—

Whoever forces another to run
prefers to walk.

—403—

The apple is not in the garden,
rather the garden the apple.

—404—

Big instrument making sounds
higher in pitch than a violin is a pig.

—405—

Discover unknown codes
through known modes.

—406—

"Crazy Horse" discovered
that a mad horse lived within
and spent the rest of his life
learning to ride it.

—407—

The final draft is a survivor's raft.

—408—

The real godhead is not a head nor a god
but the body of the two.

—409—

When placed on the floor,
a candle becomes a handle
to open an invisible door.

—410—

Surrounded by truth,
the square became a circle.

—411

Insanity is *not* reeling against inanity.

—412—

The human machine is not a mechanical
but an existential gene.

—413—

Night terror is separated from beauty
by a light error.

—414—

Free thought is not free but hard fought.

—415—

Satisfaction is the *whole* fact, not a fraction.

—416—

Define the universe in an infinite fine line.

—417—

Overcome the stupidity of flesh
to rediscover what is fresh.

—418—

The right or wrong word
cuts deeper than any sharpened sword.

—419—

Profanity is found to be not profound.

—420—

Duality is a duel between foes
unable to overcome woes.

—421—

A child is a wild adult.

An adult is the end result.

—422—

Search for the miraculous caught between

the mirage and its own stage.

—423—

Profanity in excess leads to insanity.

—424—

What makes blood for the brain

receive an energetic flood?

—425—

The wet nurses the dry earth

as a fertile purse.

—426—

Traditional relationship:

woman is the infrastructure,

man is the superstructure—

without the *infra* there is no *super.*

—427—

My name is bud. I have room to bloom.

—428—

Victim by choice negates a voice.

—429—

God *is* the plan of Man.
Man is the plan of God.

—430—

A page from the Book of Humans
turns yellow with age.

—431—

Inside the mouth is the Cosmos.
Inside the mouth of Cosmos is Chronos.

—432—

Nature is our own base we cannot erase—
there to both reflect and perfect.

—433—

It is up to the physique to absorb the strain
of the creator's pain of the mystique.

—434—

Is human life merely lukewarm,
half measure or can it be fulfilled
as full-on treasure?

—435—

Heat comes from fire,
a church from its spire.

—436—

Sourdough is the ferment
used to raise matter
in the tour through life's clatter.

—437—

Physically take a fall;
never take for granted we are tall.

—438—

Dance *is* abundance.

—439—

Heaven knocks at the door—
it's room seven.

—440—

Is the loss of reason
the Mind committing treason?

—441—

Once the words have left the mouth
they migrate south.

—442—

Praise the maize you can raise.

—443—

Song creates the work,
but takes work to make a song.

—444—

Become an instrument of the will—
kill ill-will.

—445—

Levels upon levels of quality
still does not equal equality.

—446—

Calm center of the spiral is a healing balm.

—447—

Enlighten up.

—448—

Are we the period after the last word,
or a mere point on a graph
of an opening paragraph?

—449—

The letter "o" in God is the same "o"
and second letter of *sound*
as it travels round.

—450—

Misery is blind to mystery
as the mind is blind to itself as unique find.

—451—

The only election of real worth
is the natural selection that occurs at birth.

—452—

The smile of the crocodile
is as long as the Nile is a wide mile.

—453—

Stretch the mind with a sketch,
or sketch the mind with a stretch.

—454—

Plant thoughts in the cool soil,
not leave them in the head
to heat up and boil.

—455—

Inside the factory of the dissatisfied
there are many stories left untold:
dissatisfactory.

—456—

Sound of the horn
removes the thorn of being born.

—457—

Purge, urge and surge.

—458—

Dress is another address.

—459—

Home of the artist is the dome.

—460—

Give and take, forgive and make.

—461—

Objective of the subjective is to be objective.

—462—

A race starts in place and ends in space.

—463—

Accomplish the task to answer
the one question we don't ask.

—464—

The mountain's forge contains a gorge.

—465—

Become a master—overcome disaster.

—466—

Love the tale to understand the female.

—467—

Not hearing the harmony
through the din is original sin.

—468—

A genealogical tree does not set you free.

—469—

Harboring self-doubt,
the ship of mind cannot dock.

—470—

Ore is the fine line of the seashore.

—471—

A house without walls has no halls.

—472—

A joker is the king's mood broker,
a fool from another school.

—473—

Before passivity has one completely beat
move from the passenger's
to the driver's seat.

—474—

Dozens of eyes painted
on its performing gown,
the clown is the most complete artist
who has come to town.

—475—

Believes, he lives; lies, he dies.

—476—

Peace is to play with the toy of joy
as the missing piece.

—477—

Think of the key as a vision
or use it to escape from prison.

—478—

In the shadow, the soul has no window.

—479—

Visionary image *is* the mage.

—480—

Workhorse and racehorse vie for power
throughout life's course.

—481

Somewhere between heaven and hell,
stopped in purgatory to finish the story.

—482—

Mind works more fully when it has a bully.

—483—

Death to inner voice kills outer choice.

—484—

Honest is never letting the truth rest.

—485—

Circus of Love is the flying trapeze
with no safety net as seen from above.

—486—

As the body becomes more agile
mental process is less fragile.

—487—

Dictator and genius are at opposite ends
of the spectrum of greatness.
After you conquer that world,
what do with this one?

—488—

Like quantum mechanics
happiness changes when observed.

—490—

The best medicine for man
is the Medicine Man.

—491—

The fire-eater has an angel mouth.
The flame-thrower has no name.
The sword-swallower is a man
of few words, cut down before spoken,

—492—

Sleep is for the mind. Rest is for the body.
Dream is for the soul.

—493—

A failed attempt causes self-contempt.
A successful action creates
coming attraction.

—494—

Play the word, draw the note,
picture destiny—
the future is the past presently.

—495—

House of cards ends in chards.

—496—

Can just fresh air repair
boredom, anxiety and despair?

—497—

Who is his own master needs no servant.
He serves himself.

—498—

With frequency we are a radio band,
ready to ride the right wave at hand.

—499—

Who is the breadwinner
does not need to say
how it is eaten for dinner.

—501—

Lust with no fire turns to rust.

—502—

Rather than art created for people,
people are re-created for art.

—503—

Art for art's sake is forsaken.

—504—

When consciousness is the gun,
firing it at a target can be fun.

—505—

A self-imposed prison is the second
freedom seen through a prism.

—506—

Pen is not to enclose but compose.

—507—

The further the fool travels,
the more the spool unravels.

—508—

In between scroll and paper is the codex—
what comes next?

—509—

Plato's words were not page turners
but "scroll-binding."

—510—

On a ten-scroll roll
the Platonic forms took shape.

—511—

A brush with papyrus
served to write the first opus.

—512—

The Epicurean was not epic but protean.

—513—

Humming with the drum is not humdrum.

—514—

The pen cannot contain zen.

—515—

A pencil has no faults. It can erase itself.

—516—

Focus opus.

—517—

Art can be deconstructed,
but music cannot be decomposed.

—518—

Science is encompassed by conscience,
motion by emotion.

—519—

There are no sorrows in tomorrows.

—520—

Today is in the ray.

—521—

Sun is both father *and* son.

—522—

Mishap is a gap.

—523—

A scribe can describe how a quill can thrill.

—524—

Earth is mirth, ground is sound.

—525—

Hell has no bell. Heaven has seven.
Purgatory sounds its own glory.

—526—

"Improve" changes below to above.

—527—

Color's value is its valor.

—528

Open emotional gates
to flood write with blood.

—529—

A metaphysical quilt
is a patchwork of ideas filled to the hilt.

—530—

Self-satisfaction as a whole is not a fraction,
suffering no faction.

—531—

The ultimate psychiatrist is also an artist
who can paint a better picture.

—532—

Ignore the bore, there is nothing more.

—533—

Meaning is something to see and behold,
and cannot be searched for
and found like a pot of gold,

—534—

Creatively processed
is obsessed and possessed.

—535—

Horn of plenty is filled with music,
and for this we give thanks.

—536—

For paradise roll the dice
on a planet rife with vice.

—537—

Maintain the terrain to entertain the rain.

—538—

Yearn, learn and earn—
listen to the three ears.

—539—

Laughter is the prayer without the prayer.
There is a reason why the noun and verb
are the same word.

—540—

Many gods in one, or one in many—
choose between the monad, the dyad
or their combination, the triad.

—541—

Children are punished for seeing too much.

—542—

Brothers don't fear others.
Sisters are not disasters.

—543—

Fear laughter and life is a slaughter.

—544—

Navigate the stream of consciousness
through its turbulent gate.

—545—

Those in power are not creative.
Those who are creative are not in power.
This is not the end of creation.

—546—

Discover your humanity:
imitate an animal in totality.

—547—

Overcome pain is a pleasure—
this is no plea for sure.

—548—

Those who feel the most pity
for the human race
observe it from outer space.

—549—

The iconoclast believes in image fast.

—550—

Exalt is not a fault.

—551—

Worship the ship that works.

—552—

The four horsemen are fluid
with heads of waterfall, river, lake
and sea—fall, flow stillness and current.

—553—

With arms for eyes
who could resist their charms?

—554—

Need all ancient knowledge be preserved
in the fertile seed?

—556—

Walking with feet of clay
there is no dawn to day

—558—

Inside God is man and inside man is god—
the great and the small make all.

—559—

The presence of doors and windows
is open in the house of essence.

—560—

The comic side of all tragedy
and the tragic side of all comedy.

—561—

The color wheel is always reinvented.

—562—

The eel returns to the sky in lightning.

—563—

Heights are concealed in weights.

—564—

Sky is a motion picture in living color.

—565—

The ear is nowhere but hear.

—566—

Tell the story to reinstate primal glory.

—567—

A face cannot scratch its own surface.

—568—

Plant an arm, grow a farm.

—569—

Are you a place holder or a holder of *your* place?

—570—

A game is a sport that is tame.

—571—

Give yourself away by laughing that way.

—572—

Silver river runs up the spine in a shiver.

—573—

The syntax of language seemed to follow
the same laws as celestial mechanics
even with its inherent age and flaws.

—574—

A natural plant is the plan it plants.

—575—

Free will has been pre-determined.

—576—

The outline of truth is its outline.

—577—

String a necklace of words
to ring around the world's face.

—578—

Hold the world no different
than the head of a woman bold.

—579—

Old habits are to be worn then broken.

—580—

Back to grammar:
Passive voice or active choice?

—581—

Afraid of going deep,
you are more alive when asleep.

—582—

The peacock sees all its feathers unlock.

—583—

Severed from the gods with a knife,
one leads a dog's life.

—584—

One note properly played
is worth a thousand others mislaid.

—585—

The world outside and within
is the same guide.

—586—

Search to find the ideal branch to perch.

—587—

The visionary beam
pierces the mind in a luminous gleam.

—588—

The more you write
the more you are not wrong.

—589—

Focus on "something else"
to create an opus.

—590—

Become a radar tower
by dramatically increasing candle-power.

—591—

The ultimate present
reaches beyond the present.

—592—

God never experiences "le fiasco"
when making love to his creation.

—593—

A gentleman is not always gentle.

—594—

Recover to uncover a lover.

—595—

Conquer with one's own hand
to understand.

—596—

The mate tests the ultimate.

—597—

We are homing pigeons coming home for eons.

—598—

Rise as a river, set as a sun,
swing the hammer, the work has begun.

—599—

Bronze body, golden silence, silver tongue.

—600—

Aromatic is romantic and tactic, not frantic.

—601—

Everyone who wasn't holding umbrellas
after the rain of books became well-read
from the reign of knowledge.

—602—

Those who should be censored are not
and those that shouldn't be are.
Incensed and nonsense, it makes no sense.

—603—

The sun-boat rises with the tide,
but it's the gunboat that offers the ride.

—604—

What greater foe than ego?

—605—

Project the project.

—606—

Free to sail the open sea
and fail when the storm is all one can see.

—607—

All of creation in every nation
is reincarnation.

—608—

Poetry was first spoken or sung
but now it is prose here
to propose and compose.

—609—

Try to finish the book
before you know you have started.

—610—

Wherever the battlefield,
there will be something to yield
either in men or arms to wield.

—611—

Where to follow the true Nile
for these gods now in exile?

—612—

The quantum mood is linear
and comes in waves,
changing when you notate it in staves.

—613—

Not in name but in dance,
the original artist is his own provenance.

—614—

In meditation a deal can mediate
between real and fate.

—615—

The mute of the mime
is the silent flute in our time.

—616—

Happiness is never aware of its state
while sadness proclaims its own fate.

—617—

In the kingdom of heaven
the ratio of adults to children
is one to seven.

—618—

Insight does little good
if it cannot influence the mood.
The mood does little good
if it cannot burn its own wood.

—619—

If there is no gap to bridge
why are we up here looking down
from the top of the ridge.?

—620—

Hysterical lacks mystical.
Hysteria is no mystery.
Mastery is mystery.

—621—

Does dark matter matter
or is it a light subject for the latter?

—622—

Failing along the long stairway
between heaven and hell,
there is no railing.

—623—

Road behind is dead,
what stretches ahead is a way to be fed.

—624—

A clear vision is worth the struggle
of a life of self-division.

—625—

Energy combines terrestrial
with extraterrestrial.

—626—

Drinking the Milky Way swath,
galactic man becomes the gala
of the whole path.

—627—

The difference in the circumference
between well-rounded
or in hell confounded is sanity or insanity.

—628—

Captain must be hip
to be in full control of the ship.

—629—

Train the eye to see in the rain,
hop a freight train.

—630—

Valley and mountain *peak* together.
One cannot get high without the other low.

—631—

World spins its own story.

—632—

Span the universe
has always been the plan.

—633—

The Cosmos is its own makeover.

—634—

There is no greater one than One?

—634—

As god's confidant,
the creator is not always confident.

—634—

The problem with dogma is it's not catlike.

—635—

The problem is not how to see God,
but how to not see.

—636—

The first church is the rainbow
worshipping the gods of color show.

—637—

The pineal does not opine in tone.
It is the *pinecone.*

—638—

Soul driver has good karma.

—639—

Rein*ca*mation:
To come back as a car in itself.

—640—

Under low pressure, the tire tires.

—641—

The superiority and inferiority complex
is complex.

—642—

Too much information causes deformation.

—643—

Fish were born to dine with white wine.

—644—

Don't need a brain for a life without pain.

—645—

Everyone has two sides: *right* and wrong.
Which side has been left out?

—646—

Number seven is key to universal heaven.

—648—

Feel the spike learning to like
flying the kite.

—649—

Divine right of the art critic
does not follow a basic line—it's acidic.

—650—

Can chess can make sense
out of this existential mess?

—651—

As a rough draft is a raft adrift—
with no revision or final vision.

—652—

To be brave takes courage
for freedom to crave.

—653—

The mind contains
more than it maintains it contains.

—654—

The brain maintains a negative bias
removed from its positive dais.

—655—

Will of power is still power of will.

—656—

Be skeptical of skepticism
and unsure of surety.

—657—

Hell is a mental state
not determined by fate.

—658—

Become the observer
and the observed requires no observation—
it's a sensory vacation.

—659—

Everything is full of gods,
and gods are full of everything.

—660—

Greeted by a river sent the spine a shiver.

—661—

Upstream is a *head*.

—662—

Happiness is not a means to an end
but rather and end to its own means.

—663—

Pleasure is a sure plea.

—664—

Spring is the Mind as a *spring.*

—665—

Virtue is future, past is not last.

—666—

Releasing the arrow of strife,
the bow suddenly comes to life.

—667—

Train in the rain
on cue vice becomes virtue.

—668—

A sphere is being here.
God is never flat but sharp.

—669—

Rainbow plus arrow-brush is water color.

—670—

Humans form through phases
like the moon: crescent, half, new and full.

—671—

The Spirit will not break from stretching
ingrained like an etching.

—672—

Consciously introduce the hypnogogic state
to alter fate.

—673—

Heart is a large bow of the arrow of art.

—674—

Devil trains the brain, evil is its anvil.
Pound it into sound.

—675—

Dog is a cup of tea for a thirsty flea.

—676—

Gods walked the earth in normal strides,
having nothing in common
with those whose talent hides.

—677—

The sage acts according to age.

—678—

Outline of our physical frame
is the soul line out of body it came.

—678—

The source of stream-of-consciousness
is the mouth.

—679—

Dark matter is no light matter.

—680—

The first atom in the humanity kit
was a woman not split.

—681—

Split the atom and you have a race.

—682—

There is no stigma to enigma.

—683—

The calligraphy brush
provides the ultimate rush.

—684—

The deeper the well, the higher the heaven.

—685—

Unroll the reel, feel the senses reel.

—686—

Three is so odd it became free.

—687—

Eight is infinite light and weight.

—688—

Split with a one on either side
to make odd even,
eleven ascended together with seven.

—689—

Deepen the interior, open the exterior.

—690—

Head is a door to itself.

—691—

There is no real entertainment
without attainment.

—692—

The nation is a space station.

—693—

You can only show something
if you know nothing.

—694—

The cranium is a stadium.

—695—

Try to map the gap.

—696—

A hole is at the center of whole.

—697—

Wing span *is* man.

—698—

Marriage is a compound sentence.

—699—

To be *one* is to "to be," two.

—700—

Let the sky become ground all around.

—701—

Iconic does not panic.

—702—

Let truth find *you* searching.

—703—

Where to perch
is the right post for research.

—704—

The largest color is a gray area.

—705—

Scent to the nose, a rose is present

—706—

Only upside-down
can things be understood right-side-up.

—707—

Limb knows how to climb.

—708—

God is six-sided.

—709—

Cathedral *is* music.

—710—

Rain is window to the rainbow.

—711—

Happiness is ladder, sadness its platter.

—712—

The mountain takes a peek.

—713—

With no vowel, there is no vow.

—714—

Play the pipes, plumb the depths.

—715—

In contrast we last.

—716—

If all else fails, remove the guard rails.

—717—

Decadence is missing cadence.

—718—

Original minds are both loved
and hated for the wrong reasons.

—719—

Great art makes a point at its joint.

—720—

Trust the Sacred Road of Visionary Art
to cut and thrust

—721—

Enthusiasm is the ultimate orgasm.

—722—

*Loco*motion is crazy to move.

—723—

The ultimate hill is the will.

—724—

A cow knows how to milk it,
that's the utter truth.

—725—

Thoughts exude fume or perfume.

—726—

Too much sense is nonsense,
too much nonsense makes sense.

—727—

Scared and sacred only differ in order.

—728—

Scriptures are word sculptures.

—729—

In cooking, herb is the verb.

—730—

Paranormal is the paramour of normal.

—731—

Focus on the apparatus of the opus.

—732—

Sage is passage through a dangerous age.

—732—

Pain and brain are connected in a chain.

—733—

Meaning is not found
but detected like a sound.

—734—

Insight is a knife
that cuts through everyday life.

—735—

Become yourself by being something else.

—736—

No flow, no glow.

—737—

Gods are everywhere you look
and don't look.

—738—

When inclined the ladder works.

—739—

A sheet of writing paper
is a two-way mirror.

—740—

An electrical vacation is tripped.

—741—

Lead must be led to gold.

—742—

A moment meditates
to become a minute.

—743—

The novel changed the world,
more than the world changed the novel.

—744—

Harmony is *real* money.

—745—

Ear sees more than the eye hears.

—746—

Ration the rational to determine
the right ratio.

—747—

Mainstream has two banks
with a gold dream.

—748—

Woman as waterfall rises to new heights.

—749—

Normality contains the word *mal.*

—750—

A trunk takes chances with its branches.

ABOUT THE AUTHOR

David L. Laing is a visionary self-taught artist and writer currently living and working in Seattle, Washington. His works in oil, acrylic, watercolor, and pen and ink drawing have been exhibited in South America, the United States, and Europe.

David expatriated in his early twenties and headed for South America with no money, in hopes of finding or founding a "New Paris for artists." Two months later and thirty pounds lighter, he limped into São Paulo, Brazil, having traversed the entire continent overland, nearly ten thousand miles, surviving purely on his own wits and with the aid of a few helpful souls. David spent over fifteen years in Brazil writing, painting, and composing music.

Since his return to the USA, David has focused on book publishing of his own novels, art books, and compilations of his articles. Solar Codex: A Light Odyssey and Notes from the Milky Way are the first two volumes in the quartet of Cosmic Adventure novels. At present, he is working on the other two novels to complete the quartet and is preparing for publication many new books of drawings, articles, dialogs, plays, and screenplays. Most of David's written work is lavishly illustrated with literally hundreds of drawings, all hand-inked by him.

CONNECT WITH DAVID L. LAING

PURCHASE ARTWORK

Drawings and paintings from David L. Laing's books and other themed collections may be purchased at his Cosmic Art Center page on ArtPal.com/davidllaing. His work is available as fine art prints, canvas prints, custom framed prints, and even mugs.

CONNECT ONLINE

- **Website:** Find David's books, artwork and more at www.davidllaing.com.
- **Email newsletter:** Join at www.davidllaing.com for news about book releases, art collections, exhibits, and other new projects.
- **Instagram:** Follow David at www.instagram.com/davidl.laing/.
- **Twitter:** Follow David at twitter.com/DavidLLaing9.
- **YouTube:** See book trailers and animated illustrations at www.tinyurl.com/cosmic-art-center-videos.

ARTSANA VIDEO

Watch the video of David's art book, *Artsana, 35 Sacred Yoga Asanas Expressed Through Art*, at tinyurl.com/artsana-video. Produced by One Field Media, www.onefieldmedia.com, and David L. Laing, this short film features eight extraordinary yogis, accompanied with music by Andre Feriante, www.andreferiante.com.

ALSO BY DAVID L. LAING

ART BOOKS

Higher Glyphs

Artsana: 35 Sacred Yoga Asanas Expressed Through Art

Alpha 2 Zulu: Military Alphabet Coloring Book

AlphaBetter: Coloring Book of Letters and Numbers

Ancient Runes: For Coloring and Meditation

Willing Evolution

Dance of the Dance

ANTHOLOGIES

ARTICLES

Beyond the Box, Volume 1

Beyond the Box, Volume 2

Beyond the Box, Volume 3 [Forthcoming]

Beyond the Box, Volume 4 [Forthcoming]

APHORISMS

Not Yet Human

Almost Human

Just Human

Fully Human [Forthcoming

NOVELS

COSMIC ADVENTURE QUARTET

Solar Codex: A Light Odyssey

Notes from the Milky Way

Pentagram Rising [Forthcoming]

Prometheus Reforged [Forthcoming]